MY FIRST LOOK AT VEHICLES

SHINY RED CARS LOOK SPORTY AND FUN

Cars

CATHY TATGE

CREATIVE EDUCATION

Published by Creative Education

P.O. Box 227, Mankato, Minnesota 56002

Creative Education is an imprint of The Creative Company

Designed by Rita Marshall

Photographs by AP / Wide World (Eric Risberg), Artemis Images (ATD Group, Inc.,

Indianapolis Motor Speedway, Tim O'Hara, Pikes Peak International Hill Climb), Cleo

Photography, Corbis (Giry Daniel, Duomo / William Sallaz, Tim Wrigh), Creatas, Defense

Visual Information Center, Herbert L. Gatewood, Getty Images (Michael Malyszko,

Photographer's Choice, Stone, Stringer), Ann Gordon, Sally McCrae Kuyper, Alan Look,

Doug Mitchel, National Air and Space Museum (Smithsonian Institute), Bonnie Sue Rauch,

D. Jeanene Tiner, Toyota

Printed in the United States of America

Library of Congress Cataloging-in-Publication Data

Tatge, Cathy. Cars / by Cathy Tatge

p. cm. — (My first look at vehicles)

Includes index.

ISBN-13: 978-1-58341-527-6

I. Automobiles—Juvenile literature. I. Title. II. Series.

TL I47.T3I8 2007   629.222—dc22   2006027446

First edition 9 8 7 6 5 4 3 2 I

Cars

Vroom!

Cars are vehicles that people drive on roads. They have four wheels. Some cars have two doors. Other cars have four doors. Cars have a steering wheel. The driver uses the steering wheel to turn the car.

All cars have seat belts to help keep people safe. People should always wear seat belts in cars. Seat belts can save lives.

PEOPLE HAVE TO DRIVE CARS CAREFULLY IN RAIN

People can go many places in cars. They can go to work or to school. They can go shopping or to a friend's house. Some people ride in cars every day!

The First Cars

Before people had cars, they walked. Then they used animals to take them places. Big animals like horses pulled wagons for people to ride in. But people wanted to make wagons that did not need animals.

The first car could
travel only 2.3 miles
(3.7 km) in one hour.

THIS EARLY CAR HAD ONLY THREE WHEELS

A German man named Gottlieb Daimler (*GOT-leeb DIME-ler*) made the first **motor** in 1885. Soon, people put motors on wagons. They called them cars. Now they did not need horses to pull wagons.

The first cars were very big. They could not go far. Then other people made cars that could go a long way. These cars could go much faster, too!

In the United States and
Canada, cars drive on the
right-hand side of the road.

THE FIRST CARS WERE STARTED WITH A CRANK

Cars That Work

Cars take people where they need to go. Some cars have special jobs. Only special people can drive these cars.

Racecars can go fast. People cannot drive racecars on the street. They have to drive racecars on special racetracks. The fastest racecars can go 300 miles (483 km) per hour!

Lots of people like to watch
fast cars race. A famous
race is called the Indy 500.

Police officers drive police cars. These cars have lights and sirens on top. When a police car's lights flash, other cars get out of the way.

Some cars work all day long. Taxis take people to many different places. People pay the taxi driver to take them to another place.

Big cities like New York have lots of taxis

Cars of the Future

People come up with new ideas for cars every day. They want to make cars safer to ride in. They also want to make cars better for the **environment**.

Most cars use **gasoline** to make the motor work. But now carmakers want to make cars that use less gas. This is better for the air. Some new cars use both electricity and gas.

In South America, cars use

alcohol instead of gasoline

to make their motors run.

SOME CARS USE ELECTRICITY FOR CITY DRIVING

NEW KINDS OF CARS ARE BUILT EVERY YEAR

Cars of the future may not look the same as they do today. They may also work differently. But cars will always take people where they need to go.

SOMEDAY, CARS MAY NOT NEED GAS

Hands-on: The ABC Game

The next time you are riding in a car, play this fun game with a friend or your family!

What You Need

A friend or your family

What You Do

1. Watch signs, trucks, or buildings to find a word that begins with the letter "A." Ask someone to help you say the word if you do not know what it is.
2. After everyone has found an "A" word, find a word that begins with the letter "B."
3. Continue through the alphabet. Some letters are harder to find, but the first one to "Z" wins!

GAMES CAN MAKE LONG DRIVES SEEM SHORTER

Index

Words to Know

alcohol—a liquid made from wood or grain, such as corn

environment—everything around you

gasoline—a liquid that is used to power vehicles

motor—a machine that makes a car move

Read More

Barton, Byron. *My Car*. New York: Greenwillow Books, 2001.

Dorling Kindersley Publishing Staff. *The Big Book of Things That Go*. New York: DK Publishing, 1994.

Mitton, Tony. *Cool Cars*. Boston: Kingfisher, 2005.

Explore the Web

Activities for Kids http://www.activitiesforkids.com/travel/travel_games.htm

Otto the Auto in the Otto Club http://www.ottoclub.org/

Vince & Larry's Safety City http://www.nhtsa.dot.gov/kids/